Imperfect Journeys

Peter Masters

Also by Peter Masters

The Control Book

Look Into My Eyes

Understanding BDSM Relationships

BDSM Relationships - How They Work

BDSM Relationships - Pitfalls and Obstacles

BDSM Relationships - Books 1, 2, and 3

This Curious Human Phenomenon

Cover art by Peter Masters

http://www.peter-masters.com/

ISBN 978-0-9923263-0-2

Contents

Dear diary...

Dear diary...

Morning

6:00 AM
Awoken by naked slave girl sitting on a stool next to the bed playing soothing strains of pleasant song while accompanying herself on the guitar

6:01 AM
Touch face and I realise I need a shave. Look at naked slave girl under the guitar and realise that she does also

6:02 AM
Beat slave mercilessly and left her in a twitching puddle of orgasmic ecstasy. Shame about the guitar

Dear diary...

Breakfast

6:30 AM
Slave drags herself into kitchen to prepare breakfast for her master (me). Instruct her to clean up blood smears along the floor from the bedroom once I leave

6:35 AM
Toast and jam for breakfast... well, toast. Jam jar won't open and flogging it doesn't help. It must be a SAM. At least the butter quickly melted beneath my imperious gaze

Dear diary...

Shower

6:50 AM

Shower. As usual, it's proving difficult to get the soap lather inside the latex. Maybe will try taking off the latex for tomorrow's shower

Dear diary...

Car

7:30 AM

Walk out to the car. It won't start. Go back inside to get my heaviest flogger and my stiffest riding crop. Begin to convince car to start in ways only a true submissive can fully appreciate!

7:45 AM

Have decided to go to the office by public transport

Dear diary...

Bus

7:50 AM

Start towards bus stop. People move out of my way as I walk along the pavement. My sunglasses give me a look of mystery and the white stick I bought at a charity shop serves well to indicate my rank!

8:20 AM

Bus driver was no match for my will and stopped right outside my office building at the space I indicated him, the one coincidentally marked with a bus sign

Dear diary...

Doors

8:22 AM
Building doors parted automatically as I approached.
They have learned well!

Dear diary...

Password

8:30 AM

Log in to workstation. Password: YourMaster

Dear diary...

Meeting

10:45 AM

Arrive at client office for meeting. Am 15 minutes early due to totally compliant traffic signals changing to green as I arrived at each them all along my route. No less is due, of course, to one so dominantly dominant as I

10:46 AM

As I'm shown to a comfortable waiting room by a pleasant female, she asks me if I would like tea or coffee. "Yes, scum-of-the-earth," I reply. "Bring me a tea, and no dilly-dallying!" The look of surprise on her face as she left the room told the story—she was completely unprepared to meet such a master!

11:05 AM

A different female arrived to lead me to the meeting. The earlier female would just have to deal with it when she arrived with my tea to find me gone

Dear diary...

Sandwich

1:00 PM
Went to sandwich shop to get lunch. Stared intently at lass serving behind the counter and got free extra cheese as a result

Dear diary...

Shibari

1:15 PM

Saw very appealing young Asian woman with delightful figure. Approached her, but her English must have been poor because she didn't seem to understand me. Tried holding my hands behind my back and saying, "Shibari," loudly a number of times but no reaction. Shame. She doesn't know what she's missing

Dear diary...

Elevator

1:20 PM
Totally dominated elevator so that it took me straight to my floor

Dear diary...

Chair

2:35 PM

Chair is not staying where it should and is rolling around on the carpet protector as I type. Got bondage rope out of bottom (haha!) drawer and tied lengths of rope from the table legs to the chair wheels to keep the chair in place. Am living dangerously: didn't bring safety shears to work!

2:43 PM

Fell out of chair trying to roll over to filing cabinet

Dear diary...

Photocopier

3:00 PM
Went to the photocopy room to make some copies of my latest report. The copier decided to challenge me by producing single-sided copies instead of double-sided ones. A few firm strokes of the riding crop which I keep hidden behind the toner and ink cupboard for just such situations, and some masterly manipulation of the copier's controls has brought it into line

Dear diary...

Spelling

4:00 PM
The auto-correct in the word-processor is being wearisome and insists on correcting "impravise" to "improvise"! I bitch-slapped the monitor and now it seems to be behaving. Typing is a bit slow now, but my hand should be better in a day or two

Dear diary...

Bus

5:10 PM
After leaving the office a mere flick of my wrist brought
a bus to an immediate stop right in front of me

Dear diary...

Dinner

6:00 PM

Slave has prepared dinner. She is extremely consistent and attentive to detail. The table is well laid, the glasses and the cutlery polished to a fine shine, and the lights are turned down so the flickering of the candles accentuates the baked beans on toast. Note to self: must look for cooking skills in next slave

Dear diary...

Stick

7:00 PM

Check email. More correspondence to answer about upcoming workshop I'm running. It's only been advertised for a month and already there are three enrolments. Topic is "Advanced control of your slave. Bring own slave and stick." One guy who contacted me only has a stick, but I said he could come along anyway

Dear diary...

Remote

7:30 PM
Batteries in TV remote control are dead so fit remote-control electric dog training collar to slave and place her next to the TV. Almost as good, but the strangled cries as I change channel or adjust the volume are a little distracting

Dear diary...

Fire

8:30 PM

Call slave into the dungeon because I have decided to do fire play scene with her

8:40 PM

Tell slave not to worry and that she can wear a wig until it grows back

My journal...

My journal...

Blindfold

Slave has been insisting that I try a blindfold with her. So I tried one. I fell over the spanking bench and hurt myself.

My journal...

Paddle

My hand gets sore when I do too much spanking so I decided I would get a paddle. Oddly, you can't just get one paddle. I had to get the whole kayak and now I don't know where to leave it.

My journal...

Negotiation

I decided to do a scene with a new submissive. We started out with the requisite negotiation, as all good masters do, and she gave me an excellent price.

My journal...

Warm-up

Someone told me that doing a warm-up with slave is important before doing something intense like heavy spanking so I make her run up and down the stairs a few times before we start.

My journal...

Schoolgirl

Schoolgirl role play with slave today. Made her learn the Gross Domestic Product of all the OECD nations. Not as hot as I thought it would be.

My journal...

Spreader bars

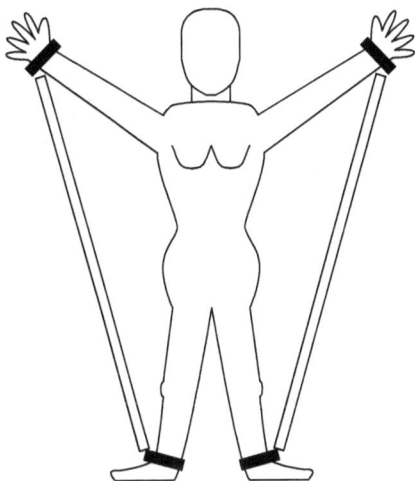

Attached slave to spreader bars like this. Now she walks funny.

My journal...

Open wide

I have acquired a device which I can insert in slave's cunt to spread her lips and open her up wide. The girl's been around the block a few times so there was a bit of an echo.

My journal...

Police

Decided to wear the "scrubs" I use in medical play on the way to work and then change at the office. As expected, this attracted much attention and admiring gazes. Even a passing police patrol took an interest, though they seemed more interested in the large blood stains than the actual outfit. Note to self: must wash scrubs more often. After courteously examining my person and discovering some old scalpels and a short length of rope I had inadvertently left in a pocket, they invited me down to the station where they did some medical play of their own.

My journal...

Wheel

Brief outing to get a snack. Note to self: Wartenberg Wheels are not ideal for cutting pizza slices.

My journal...

Super

Have decided that slave needs more challenges. Am changing safeword to "Supercalifragilisticexpialidocious".

My journal...

Torture

Trying new breast torture technique. Have taken headphones, rotated the cups and duct-taped one headphone cup to each boob on slave. Am playing Best of Roy Orbison through the headphones to see how long the boobs can take it.

My journal...

Metal

Have read about a new metal bondage technique in our local newsletter and am keen to try it once I can get a staple gun. Slave doesn't seem keen.

My journal...

Cock

Last night's party was a blast and I'm still recovering. Someone suggested cock-and-ball torture to me but I told them I'm not into animal play and that I really don't think animal cruelty has a place in BDSM.

My journal...

Musical

Half way through last night's party someone asked if I'd like to try some urethral play. I said that that I'm not very musical myself but that slave can play the guitar. That didn't seem to be the style of music they were talking about so they went to look for someone else.

My journal...

Humiliation

Humiliation play today: have instructed slave to call telephone numbers at random and when someone answers say, "What do a dog and a telephone have in common? They both have collar ID!", then hang up.

My journal...

Age play

Tried age play with slave and told her to pretend she's a teenager. Not very good results. She just became very, very annoying.

My journal...

Cage

Slave is using my cage to hang up clothes to dry. I am concerned this will cause premature rusting.

My journal...

Hog-tie

Tried to do a hog-tie but it got away.

My journal...

Violet

Have heard people raving about violet wants and wanted to get in on the action. Went to my local BDSM Equipage And Stationery store in Dubious Street and the nice man there explained it all to me and then helped me select a good quality one. I am looking forward to trying it out but, when you get down to it, it's just a purple stick and I really don't see how it'll be much better than my brown flogger.

My journal...

Denial

Am experimenting with sexual denial. Slave keeps saying it exists, and I keep saying it doesn't.

My journal...

Submit

Slave keeps saying that she truly and deeply wants to submit, and I keep telling her to write something thoughtful and send it to the local newspaper but she never does. Strange!

My journal...

Impact

Have just learned that impact play doesn't include throwing slave against a wall.

My journal...

Mummification

Tried mummification, but after I'd got slave's brain out through her nose I had a lot of trouble getting it back in again at the end of the scene. Slave hasn't been very talkative since then either.

My journal...

Fear

Another dominant mentioned that fear can be very arousing for a slave so as very naked slave was coming out of the bedroom I leapt in front of her and yelled, "Boo!," as loudly as I could. Now have brown stain on carpet.

My journal...

Caning

Tried caning with slave. It was pleasant and very social, and we now have two very nice baskets. I think I'll use mine for fruit.

My journal...

Enlightenment

Was talking with another master about enlightenment. I said unless I'm doing a medical scene and need it very bright, that I prefer endarkenment in my dungeon.

My journal...

One

A new girl approached me at the party last night and said, "One would like to be of service." I replied, "Does your master number you and your sisters?"

About the author

Peter Masters is an Australian author and BDSM-ophile. He lives in Sydney. He has been a passionate devotee of controlling the fairer sex for well over 30 years.

He has published a number of books on BDSM and on hypnosis and sex. Generally what he writes is quite serious, but then you get a book like this that spoils a pretty good record.

His main website is:

> http://www.peter-masters.com/

He has been writing about BDSM, and running workshops and discussion groups for more than 15 years.

At this very moment he doesn't feel like writing any more about himself...